HIP-HOP AND SOCIAL JUSTICE

RHYMES OF RESISTANCE

Dr. Monica B. Morall-Baker
Cicely Lewis, Executive Editor

LERNER PUBLICATIONS ◆ MINNEAPOLIS

LETTER FROM CICELY LEWIS

Dear Reader,

Hip-hop has been a part of my life from an early age. I remember using my brush as a microphone and rapping along with Salt-N-Pepa. Hip-hop influenced my fashion, way of speaking, and lifestyle. As a teacher, I shared Tupac's writings to teach poetry elements and Queen Latifah's "U.N.I.T.Y." to help my students better understand the works of poet Maya Angelou.

CICELY LEWIS

As a librarian, I want to expose my students to literature that empowers them to take action and that amplifies voices of underrepresented groups. That is what hip-hop does. Hip-hop is more than beats and rhymes; it's a cultural force. For Black people, it's been a spotlight on social justice, and a canvas for our frustrations, joys, and creativity.

As you read the series, think about the power of hip-hop and how it all began. You've probably heard of Cardi B and Nicki Minaj, but who paved the way for them? Reflect on how this musical genre that began in the Black Community is now present around the world.

—Cicely Lewis, Executive Editor

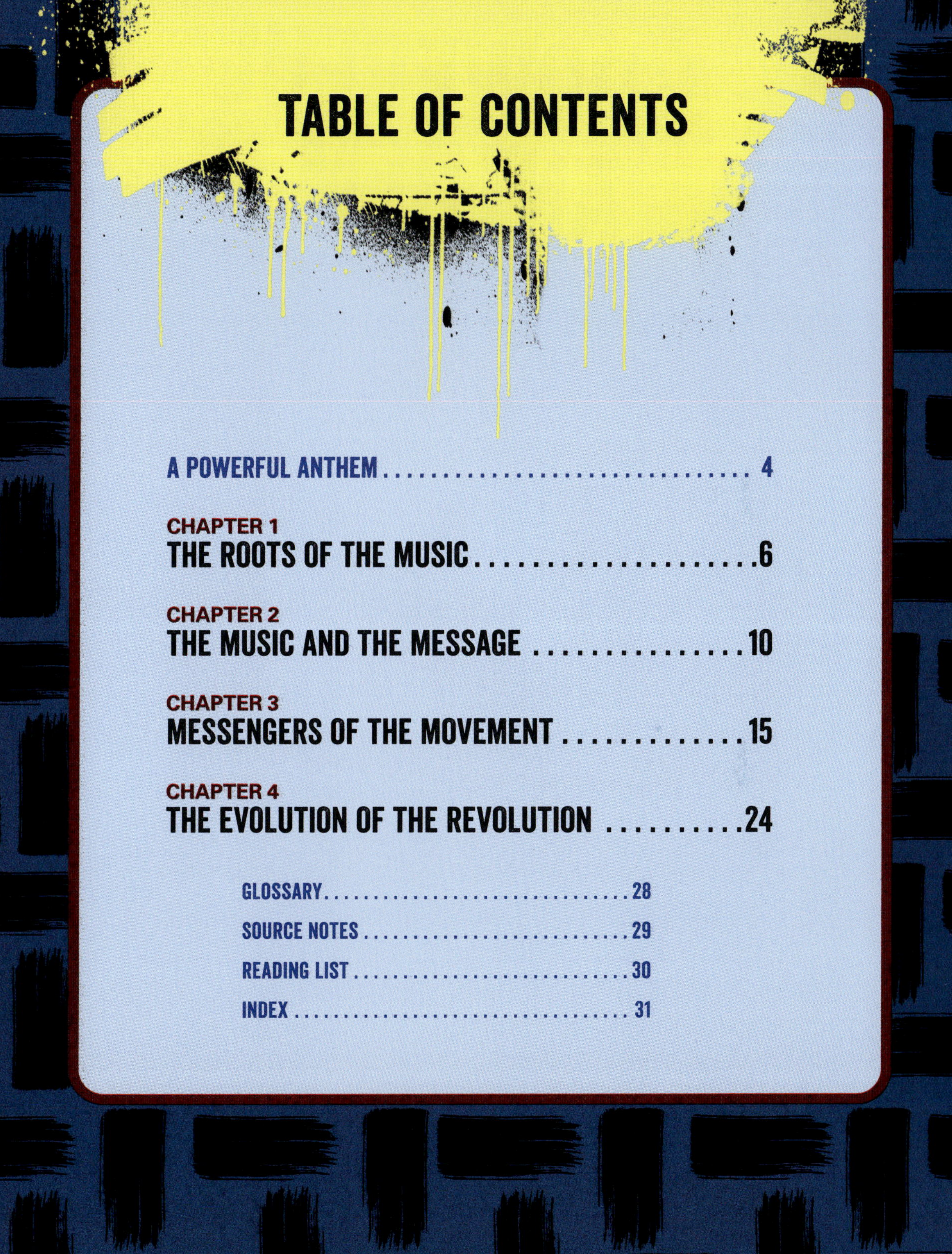

TABLE OF CONTENTS

A POWERFUL ANTHEM

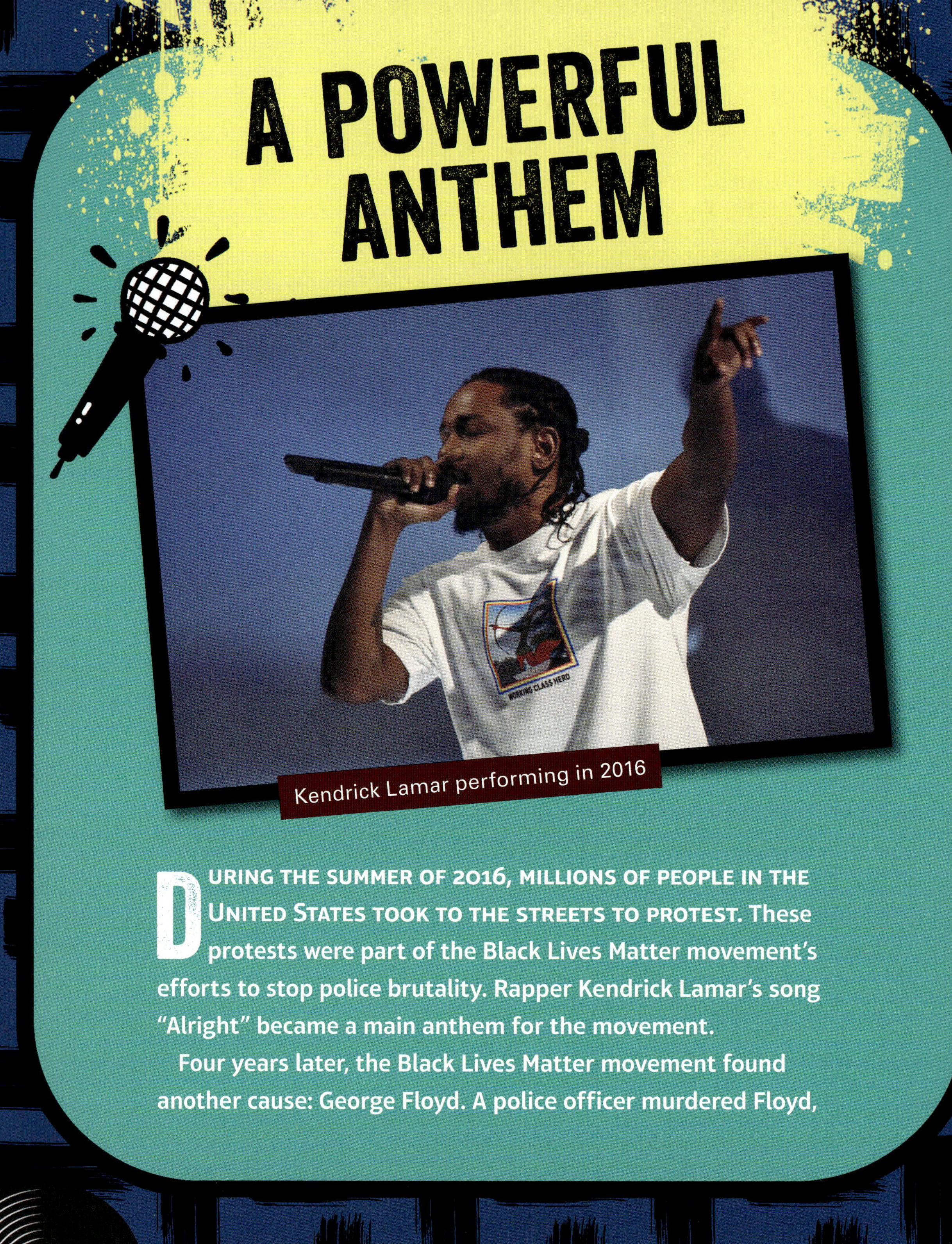

Kendrick Lamar performing in 2016

DURING THE SUMMER OF 2016, MILLIONS OF PEOPLE IN THE UNITED STATES TOOK TO THE STREETS TO PROTEST. These protests were part of the Black Lives Matter movement's efforts to stop police brutality. Rapper Kendrick Lamar's song "Alright" became a main anthem for the movement.

Four years later, the Black Lives Matter movement found another cause: George Floyd. A police officer murdered Floyd,

In 2016 people across the country marched in solidarity with the Black Lives Matter movement.

an unarmed Black man. People once again took to the streets to the sounds of Lamar's song, demonstrating the strong relationship between hip-hop music and social justice.

Hip-hop has long been the voice of marginalized youth, particularly Black and brown youth in urban areas. From the beginning, hip-hop has been an important force in the fight for social justice.

CHAPTER 1

THE ROOTS OF THE MUSIC

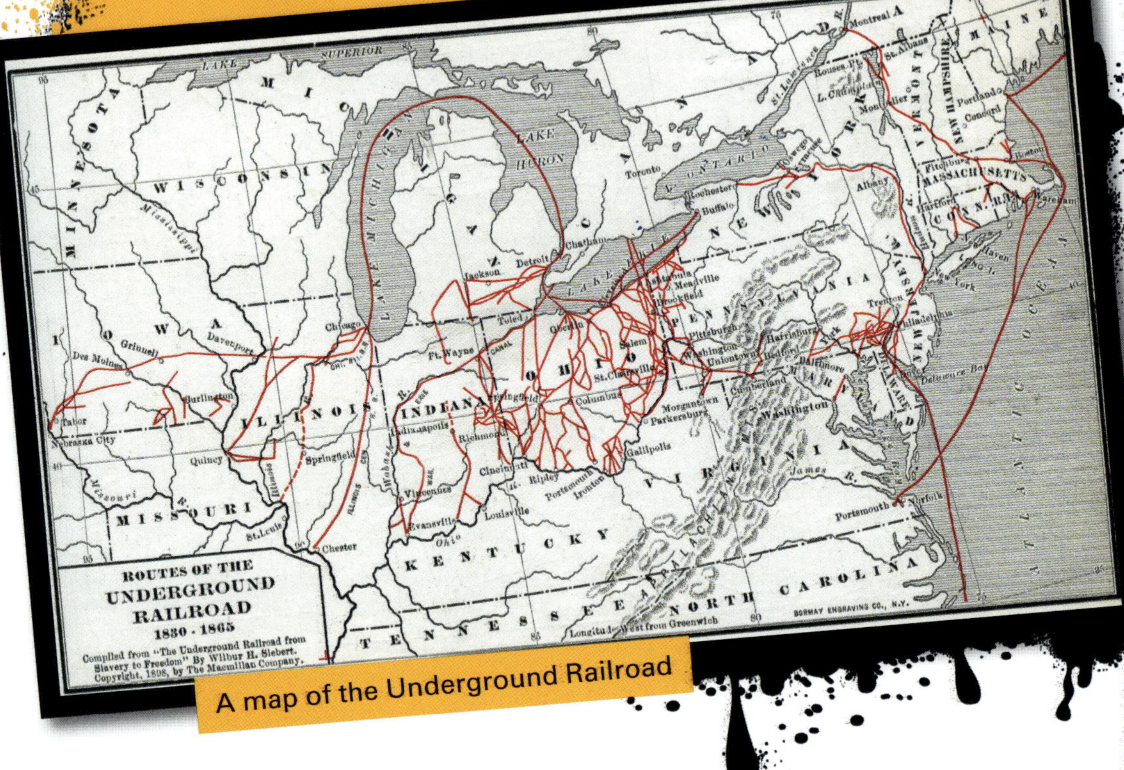

A map of the Underground Railroad

THROUGHOUT HISTORY, MUSIC HAS BEEN A POWERFUL AND UNITING FORCE FOR PEOPLE. Hip-hop music in particular has often been used as a way to identify issues in society and unite people around common goals.

SEEDS OF UNITY

During the 1800s, many enslaved people escaped slavery by going to Northern states where they could be free. One way they escaped was by using the Underground Railroad. This was a network of secret routes and safe houses that people could use to travel north. People passed secret messages about the Underground Railroad using spirituals, a type of religious folksong that enslaved Black people in the US created. The spirituals' themes of freedom would later be included in modern hip-hop music.

Harriet Tubman was a conductor for the Underground Railroad. She helped lead enslaved individuals to the North.

THE PEOPLE'S PROTEST

The Civil Rights Movement took place in the 1950s and 1960s. People protested segregation and discrimination against Black people. They also protested Black people not having the right to vote. Anthems of protest, such as "We Shall Overcome," were a way to bring attention to unfair treatment of Black Americans.

In 2014 rappers Common and Rhymefest, along with singer John Legend, wrote the song "Glory." It became the theme song

Over 250,000 people attended the March on Washington in 1963. The march advocated for the rights of Black Americans.

Common (*left*) and John Legend win the Academy Award for Best Original Song in 2015 for "Glory."

for *Selma*, a movie about civil rights marches in Alabama in the 1960s. The song honored those who fought for equal rights for people of color.

REFLECT

Music has been a big part of many movements in history. Why do you think hip-hop music plays such an important role in social justice movements?

CHAPTER 2

THE MUSIC AND THE MESSAGE

Grandmaster Flash (*center*) and the Furious Five in 1980

HIP-HOP ARTISTS AND GROUPS OFTEN USE THEIR TALENT, ART, AND PLATFORMS TO HIGHLIGHT ISSUES IN SOCIETY AND ADVOCATE FOR SOCIAL REFORM.

ILLUMINATING THE ISSUES

Many rap songs have political messages. One of the most iconic anthems in hip-hop history is the 1982 song "The Message" by Grandmaster Flash and the Furious Five. The song addresses economic issues and violence that people faced in urban areas. It was one of the first rap songs to talk about social issues.

Public Enemy's song "Fight the Power" was a powerful anthem in the late 1980s. It was written for *Do the Right Thing*, a movie directed by Spike Lee that takes place in Brooklyn, New York. The song highlighted racism and police brutality and urged people to fight against it.

After Public Enemy released "Fight the Power" in June 1989, the song hit number one on the Hot Rap Singles chart.

A HIP-HOP FIRST

In 2018 Kendrick Lamar won the Pulitzer Prize for Music. He is the only hip-hop artist to ever win this award. This was also the first time that the award was given to a genre of music that wasn't classical or jazz.

Lamar holding the certificate for the Pulitzer Prize for Music

Childish Gambino released the song "This Is America" in 2018. Similar to Kendrick Lamar's "Alright," the song forced people to look at police brutality. The music video also drew attention to rising gun violence in the United States. The song called out racial and economic inequalities in the country.

Childish Gambino performing in 2017

THE LADIES SPEAK

Hip-hop artist Ms. Melodie helped write lyrics for many songs. One of them was the 1991 hit "Heal Yourself." The song featured many artists such as KRS-One, MC Lyte, and Queen Latifah. Each artist touched on different issues, including the dangers of drug abuse and the importance of female empowerment.

Ms. Melodie (*back center*) was part of a hip-hop group called Boogie Down Productions along with rappers Willie D (*left*), KRS-One (*right*), and McBoo (*front*).

Queen Latifah (*left*) performing onstage with Monie Love during the 2018 Essence Festival in New Orleans, Louisiana

In 1989 Queen Latifah collaborated with British rapper Monie Love. The two wrote a song called "Ladies First." The lyrics promoted sisterhood and called attention to apartheid, a system of segregating Black and white people in South Africa. In 1993 Queen Latifah's song "U.N.I.T.Y." presented a message of togetherness, especially among women and families.

ICONIC INFLUENCER

Some people argue that Kendrick Lamar is one of the most influential voices in recent years. He creates songs that bring awareness to issues such as gun violence, police reform, and discrimination. Many of his songs have become anthems for social movements such as Black Lives Matter. In 2016 the rapper helped write and was featured on Beyoncé's song "Freedom." The song's lyrics talk about the inequalities Black women face, as well as police brutality in Black communities.

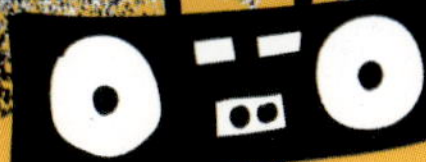

CHAPTER 3

MESSENGERS OF THE MOVEMENT

Left to right: Rappers Harmony, Ms. Melodie, and DJ D-Nice attend an album release party for Kool Moe Dee in 1991.

MANY ARTISTS USE THEIR PLATFORMS TO BOTH MOVE THE CROWD AND ENACT THE CHANGE THEY WANT TO SEE IN THE WORLD.

COMING TOGETHER

KRS-One founded a group called Stop the Violence Movement in the 1980s. Members of the group included big stars such as Kool Moe Dee, Ms. Melodie, and MC Lyte. They recorded the song "Self-Destruction" and donated a portion of the song's proceeds to the National Urban League. This group helps provide relief and educational opportunities for people in underserved communities.

In 2005 Hurricane Katrina struck the US coast near Louisiana, Mississippi, and Florida. Hip-hop artist Yasiin Bey, formerly known as Mos Def, wrote a song for the victims of Hurricane Katrina. He also held an event to raise money to help them.

Yasiin Bey performing onstage in 2018

Jay-Z (*left*) and Meek Mill (*center*) attending the launch of REFORM Alliance in 2019

MOVERS AND SHAKERS

Hip-hop superstar Jay-Z's record label Roc Nation founded the nonprofit organization United Justice Coalition. In 2019 Jay-Z partnered with rapper Meek Mill and other celebrities to create REFORM Alliance. This group brings awareness to social justice issues such as police corruption and prison reform.

"I'm here to speak for all the people who don't have a voice."

—Meek Mill, 2019

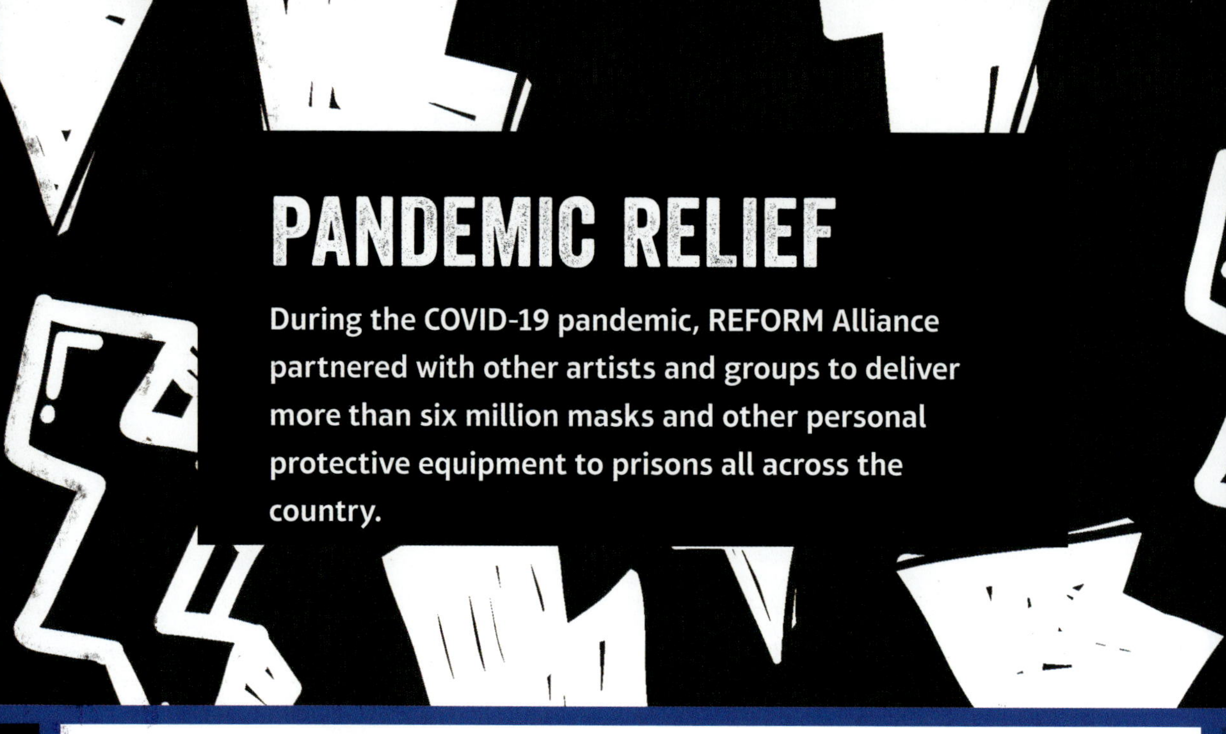

PANDEMIC RELIEF

During the COVID-19 pandemic, REFORM Alliance partnered with other artists and groups to deliver more than six million masks and other personal protective equipment to prisons all across the country.

BRINGING IN BUSINESS

Michael Render, a.k.a. "Killer Mike," is a Grammy award-winning rapper and community activist. He works with local and national leaders to support Black businesses. In 2018 Render partnered

REFLECT

Many hip-hop artists use their platform to bring attention to an issue that is important to them. If you had a platform like theirs, what issue would you raise awareness for?

Killer Mike (*left*) shaking hands with T.I. at the HOPE Global Forums in 2022

with fellow rapper T.I. to create businesses in their hometown and hired locals to work there. He also cofounded Greenwood, a company that helps Black and Latinx people manage their money.

"Now is the time to plot, plan, strategize, organize, and mobilize."

—Killer Mike, 2020

AN ADVOCATE FOR WOMEN

Megan Thee Stallion is a proud advocate for women's rights. She works with national organizations to advocate for equal access to health care for women of color.

Megan Thee Stallion talks to students at Texas State University in 2023.

"A lot of people relate to me and follow me because they want to see how I'm dressed, they want to see my lifestyle. So I feel like I have a responsibility to also share to them like, 'Hey, while you here and you're checking my outfit and checking my music, check out what's going on over here in this part of the world.'"

—Cardi B, 2022

A POWERFUL PLATFORM

Rapper Cardi B encourages young people to register to vote and make their voices heard. She uses her social media platform to speak about issues. In 2023 she called out politicians over policies she thought were unfair. She challenged them for cutting money to schools and other public services. She also donated money to her middle school and COVID-19 relief. She challenged others to donate too.

Cardi B performing at BET Experience in 2024

TAKING THE LEAD

Rapper Da Brat is a leading LGBTQIA+ artist in hip-hop. She regularly performs at concerts for charities and works with organizations such as the Make-A-Wish Foundation, a group that grants wishes to critically ill children. She also supports the Ludacris Foundation, which helps children in urban areas.

Da Brat performing in March 2021

Blanco attends the OUTLOUD: Raising Voices concert series, an event for LGBTQIA+ and allied musicians, in 2021.

SELF-CARE AND SOCIAL ACTIVISM

Rap artists such as Mykki Blanco and Angel Haze use their platforms to speak about issues such as gender identity, race, and health care. Blanco encouraged fans to support a campaign that donated money

Noname hits the stage in Austin, Texas, for a music festival in 2018.

to help unhoused Black women. Angel Haze was part of a charity that protects orphans in India and Africa.

Poet and rap artist Noname advocates for supporting mental health and protests violence against Black women. She also sponsors the Noname Book Club. This book club supports local bookstores owned by people of color to increase diverse book choices for readers.

CHAPTER 4

THE EVOLUTION OF THE REVOLUTION

Hip-hop can help transform the classroom into a critical-thinking space.

HIP-HOP CULTURE WAS BORN FROM A NEED FOR BLACK AND BROWN PEOPLE TO BE ABLE TO EXPRESS THEIR FEELINGS ABOUT THE WORLD AROUND THEM. Artists, schools, and leaders use hip-hop to help educate fans and encourage them to become advocates for important social issues.

A school in Boston, Massachusetts, holds a hip-hop class during its summer program.

PREPARE TO BE SCHOOLED

Hip-hop is becoming more widely accepted in mainstream education. Teachers use music, rhythm, and rhymes to make learning more interesting and to form cultural connections with students. Some schools offer hip-hop classes or blend hip-hop into the lessons. Language arts classes compare classic poetry to

REFLECT

Many schools view hip-hop as a helpful tool in education. How would you like to see hip-hop used in the classroom?

rap lyrics. Music classes invite local rappers and producers to talk about jobs in music. Sometimes teachers allow students to use elements of hip-hop, such as rap or dance, for school projects.

HEALING WITH HIP-HOP

Mental health therapists are always looking for new ways to engage and help patients. One type of therapy is hip-hop therapy. Therapists use hip-hop culture to connect with patients in new ways, such as making art and creating or listening to hip-hop music. It is a creative way for people who might struggle with their emotions or have trouble discussing issues to express themselves.

POLITICAL PARTNERSHIPS

When Barack Obama was president, he often invited hip-hop artists such as Kendrick Lamar, Nicki Minaj, and Ludacris to the White House. Sometimes they were there to perform. But

REFLECT

Many political leaders embrace the hip-hop community. What unique perspectives do hip-hop fans have that can help politicians?

President Barack Obama (*right*) shaking hands with Kendrick Lamar during an Independence Day celebration in 2016

other times, they discussed issues that affect underrepresented groups, such as criminal justice reform and mental health.

GETTING INVOLVED

Being an activist is not just for famous artists. Many hip-hop fans use the culture to express, educate, and advocate for themselves. There are many ways to use hip-hop culture to create positive change. Hip-hop music continues to unite with the message of justice for all.

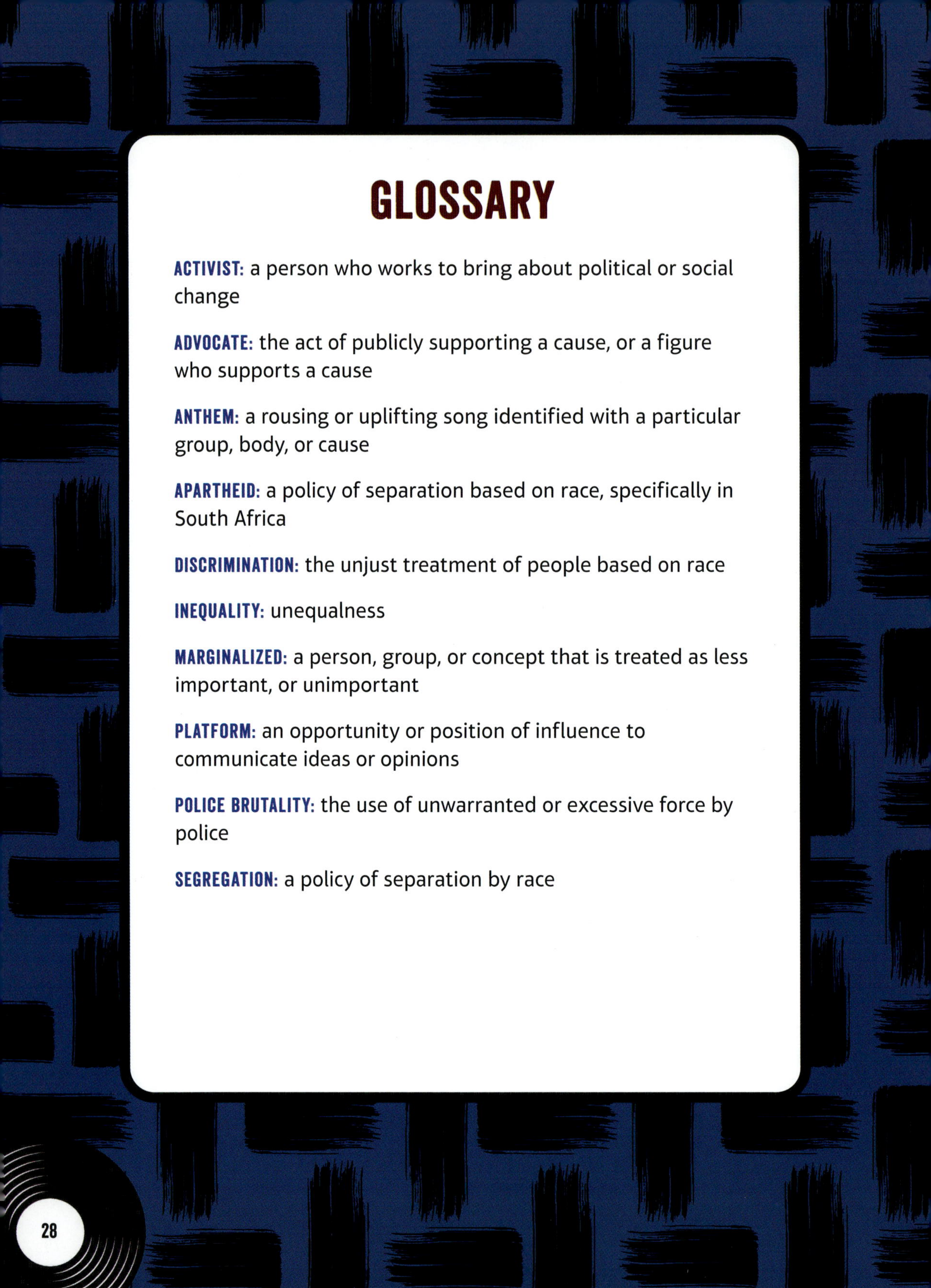

GLOSSARY

ACTIVIST: a person who works to bring about political or social change

ADVOCATE: the act of publicly supporting a cause, or a figure who supports a cause

ANTHEM: a rousing or uplifting song identified with a particular group, body, or cause

APARTHEID: a policy of separation based on race, specifically in South Africa

DISCRIMINATION: the unjust treatment of people based on race

INEQUALITY: unequalness

MARGINALIZED: a person, group, or concept that is treated as less important, or unimportant

PLATFORM: an opportunity or position of influence to communicate ideas or opinions

POLICE BRUTALITY: the use of unwarranted or excessive force by police

SEGREGATION: a policy of separation by race

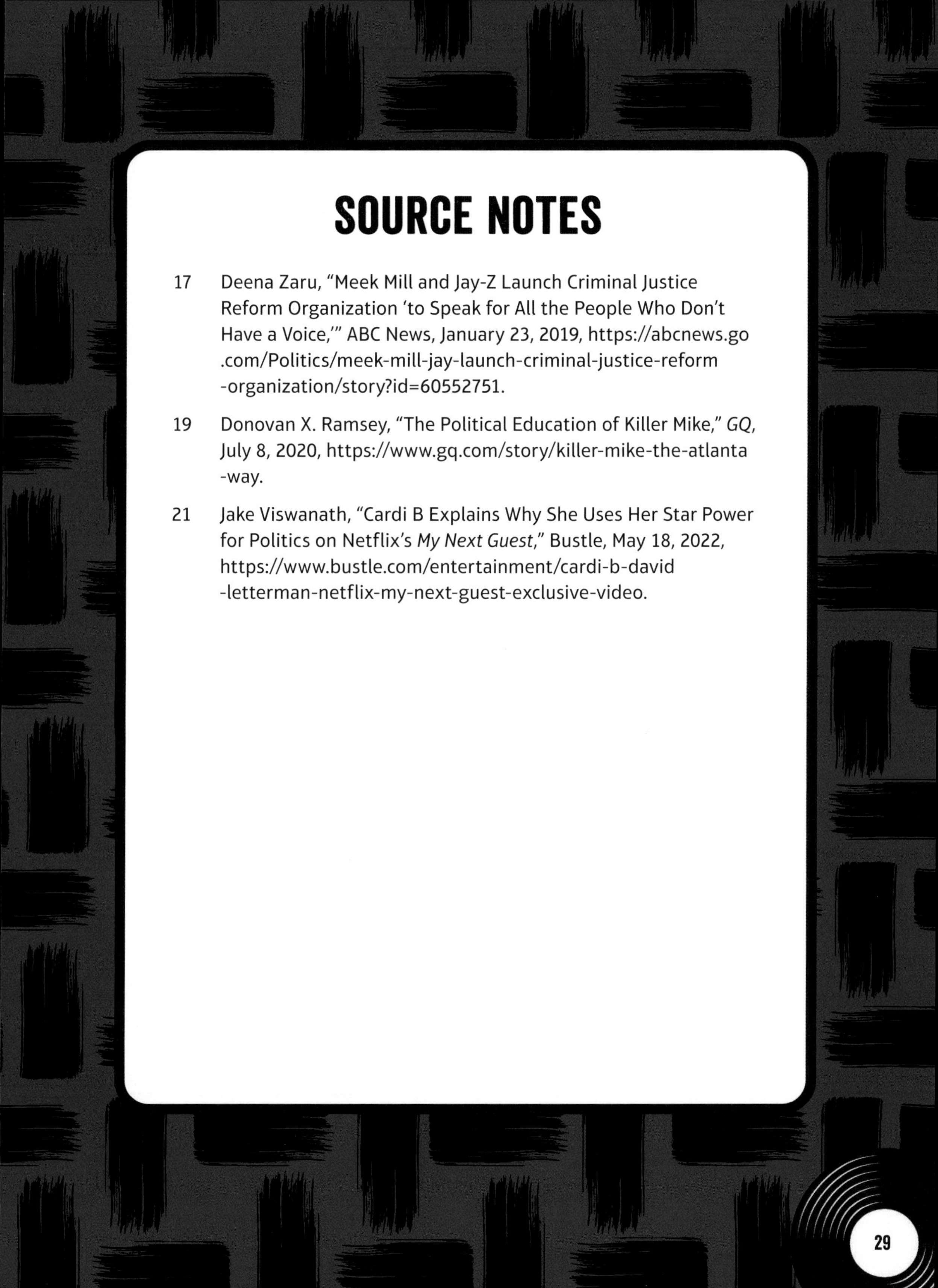

SOURCE NOTES

17 Deena Zaru, "Meek Mill and Jay-Z Launch Criminal Justice Reform Organization 'to Speak for All the People Who Don't Have a Voice,'" ABC News, January 23, 2019, https://abcnews.go.com/Politics/meek-mill-jay-launch-criminal-justice-reform-organization/story?id=60552751.

19 Donovan X. Ramsey, "The Political Education of Killer Mike," *GQ*, July 8, 2020, https://www.gq.com/story/killer-mike-the-atlanta-way.

21 Jake Viswanath, "Cardi B Explains Why She Uses Her Star Power for Politics on Netflix's *My Next Guest*," Bustle, May 18, 2022, https://www.bustle.com/entertainment/cardi-b-david-letterman-netflix-my-next-guest-exclusive-video.

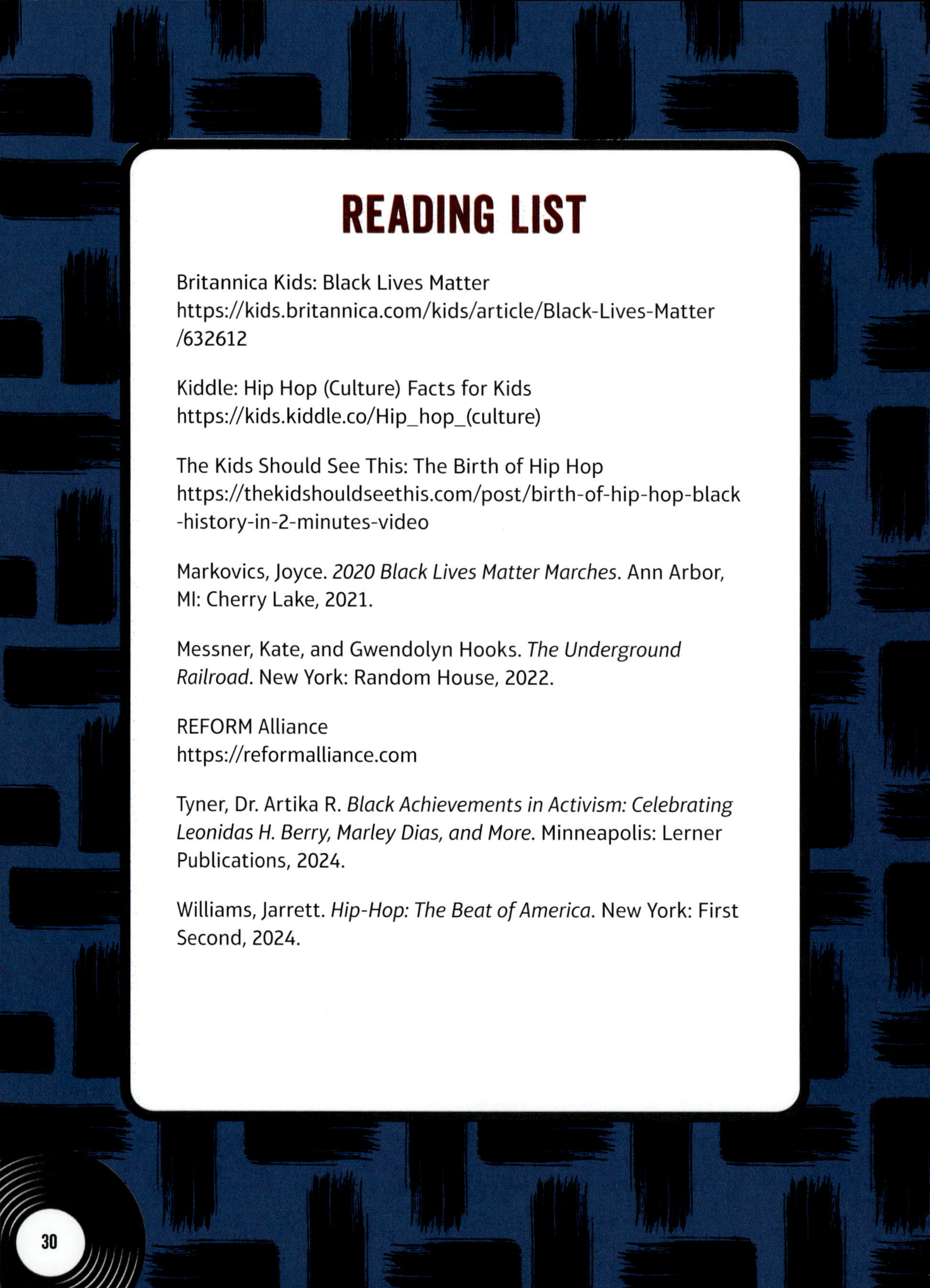

READING LIST

Britannica Kids: Black Lives Matter
https://kids.britannica.com/kids/article/Black-Lives-Matter/632612

Kiddle: Hip Hop (Culture) Facts for Kids
https://kids.kiddle.co/Hip_hop_(culture)

The Kids Should See This: The Birth of Hip Hop
https://thekidshouldseethis.com/post/birth-of-hip-hop-black-history-in-2-minutes-video

Markovics, Joyce. *2020 Black Lives Matter Marches*. Ann Arbor, MI: Cherry Lake, 2021.

Messner, Kate, and Gwendolyn Hooks. *The Underground Railroad*. New York: Random House, 2022.

REFORM Alliance
https://reformalliance.com

Tyner, Dr. Artika R. *Black Achievements in Activism: Celebrating Leonidas H. Berry, Marley Dias, and More*. Minneapolis: Lerner Publications, 2024.

Williams, Jarrett. *Hip-Hop: The Beat of America*. New York: First Second, 2024.

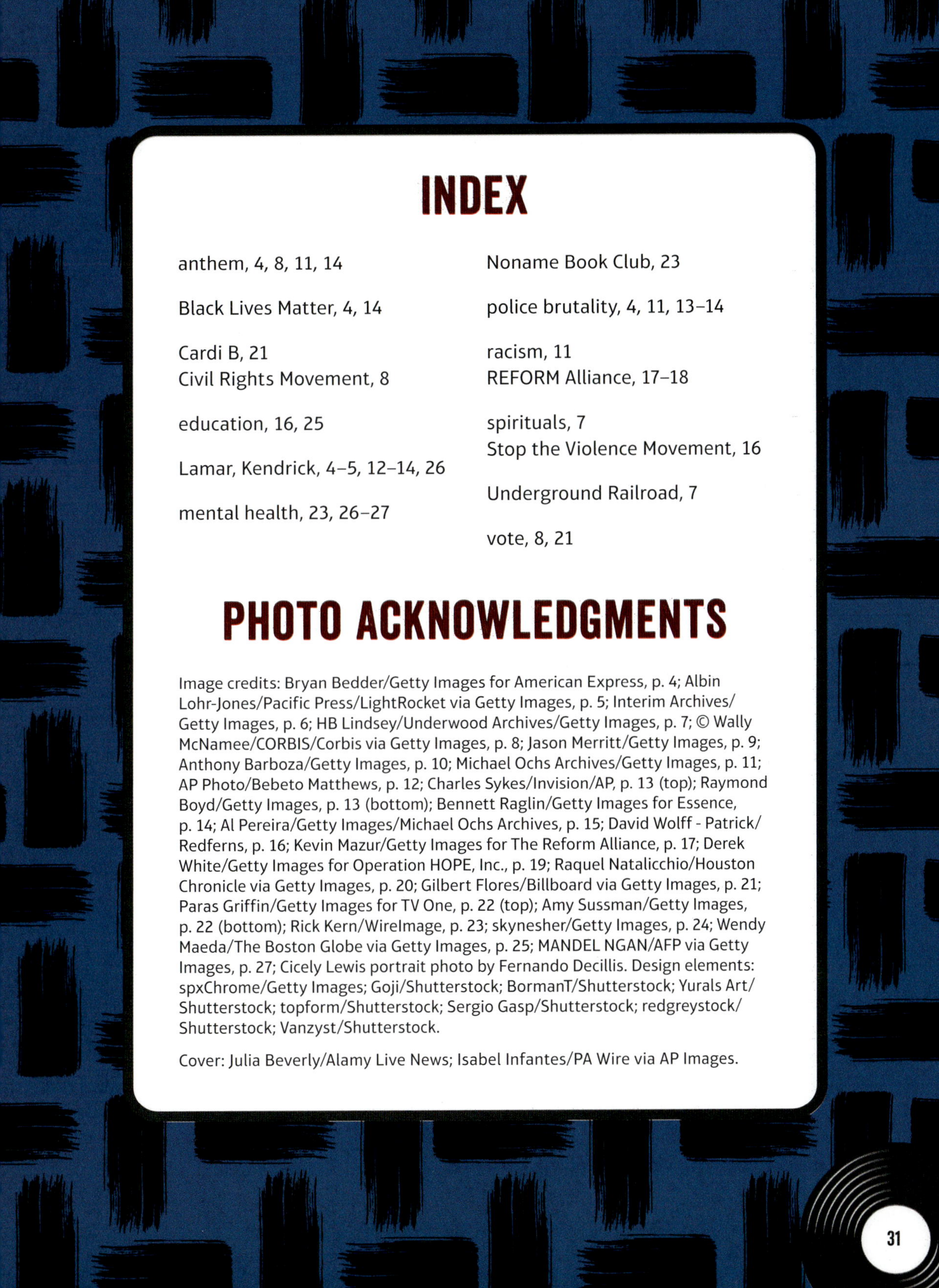

INDEX

PHOTO ACKNOWLEDGMENTS

Image credits: Bryan Bedder/Getty Images for American Express, p. 4; Albin Lohr-Jones/Pacific Press/LightRocket via Getty Images, p. 5; Interim Archives/Getty Images, p. 6; HB Lindsey/Underwood Archives/Getty Images, p. 7; © Wally McNamee/CORBIS/Corbis via Getty Images, p. 8; Jason Merritt/Getty Images, p. 9; Anthony Barboza/Getty Images, p. 10; Michael Ochs Archives/Getty Images, p. 11; AP Photo/Bebeto Matthews, p. 12; Charles Sykes/Invision/AP, p. 13 (top); Raymond Boyd/Getty Images, p. 13 (bottom); Bennett Raglin/Getty Images for Essence, p. 14; Al Pereira/Getty Images/Michael Ochs Archives, p. 15; David Wolff - Patrick/Redferns, p. 16; Kevin Mazur/Getty Images for The Reform Alliance, p. 17; Derek White/Getty Images for Operation HOPE, Inc., p. 19; Raquel Natalicchio/Houston Chronicle via Getty Images, p. 20; Gilbert Flores/Billboard via Getty Images, p. 21; Paras Griffin/Getty Images for TV One, p. 22 (top); Amy Sussman/Getty Images, p. 22 (bottom); Rick Kern/WireImage, p. 23; skynesher/Getty Images, p. 24; Wendy Maeda/The Boston Globe via Getty Images, p. 25; MANDEL NGAN/AFP via Getty Images, p. 27; Cicely Lewis portrait photo by Fernando Decillis. Design elements: spxChrome/Getty Images; Goji/Shutterstock; BormanT/Shutterstock; Yurals Art/Shutterstock; topform/Shutterstock; Sergio Gasp/Shutterstock; redgreystock/Shutterstock; Vanzyst/Shutterstock.

Cover: Julia Beverly/Alamy Live News; Isabel Infantes/PA Wire via AP Images.

FOR MOM AND DAD, AND TO DWIGHT, MY LOVE

Lerner Publications Company
An imprint of Lerner Publishing Group, Inc.
241 First Avenue North
Minneapolis, MN 55401 USA

For reading levels and more information, look up this title at www.lernerbooks.com.

Main body text set in Aptifer Sans LT Pro.
Typeface provided by Linotype AG.

Editor: Annie Zheng **Photo Editor:** Lucien Brinkley
Lerner team: Martha Kranes

Library of Congress Cataloging-in-Publication Data

Names: Morall-Baker, Monica B., author.
Title: Hip-hop and social justice : rhymes of resistance / Dr. Monica B. Morall-Baker.
Description: Minneapolis : Lerner Publications, 2025. | Series: Hip-hop culture | Includes bibliographical references and index. | Audience: Ages 9–14 | Audience: Grades 4–6 | Summary: "Hip-hop has long been at the center of social justice issues, such as civil rights, protests against police brutality, and more. From powerful anthems to influential voices, learn more about hip-hop and social justice"— Provided by publisher.
Identifiers: LCCN 2024042674 (print) | LCCN 2024042675 (ebook) | ISBN 9798765659861 (library binding) | ISBN 9798765684238 (paperback) | ISBN 9798765678091 (epub)
Subjects: LCSH: Rap (Music)—Political aspects—United States—Juvenile literature. | Hip-hop—Juvenile literature. | Social justice—United States—Juvenile literature.
Classification: LCC ML3918.R37 R672 2025 (print) | LCC ML3918.R37 (ebook) | DDC 306.4/8424—dc23/eng/20241101

LC record available at https://lccn.loc.gov/2024042674
LC ebook record available at https://lccn.loc.gov/2024042675

Manufactured in the United States of America
1-1011687-53633-2/19/2025